Projection Machine

Debrah Morkun

BlazeVOX [books]

Buffalo, New York

Projection Machine by Debrah Morkun

Copyright © 2010

Published by BlazeVOX [books]

Printed in the United States of America

Book design by Geoffrey Gatza
Cover photograph: Melissa Purnell
First Edition
ISBN: 9781935402923
Library of Congress Control Number 2009941031

BlazeVOX [books]
303 Bedford Ave
Buffalo, NY 14216

Editor@blazevox.org

publisher of weird little books

BlazeVOX [books]

blazevox.org

2   4   6   8   0   9   7   5   3   1

B   X

Acknowledgments

I would like to thank the editors of *Parcel* and *Moria* where some of the poems in this book found previous homes. I would also like to thank The New Philadelphia Poets, my sister Dyanna, Marion Bell, the roses in full bloom, the nurse in my kerchief, the saw dust in the membrane, the fools who listen to the turning tropics. Beyond this, I would like to thank Melissa Purnell, Francesca Costanzo, the poets in the sky, the falling pigeon rain clouds and the gerrymandered trails on the buffalo express. Of course I would like to thank Geoffrey Gatza, the piazza on the other side of the river, and the light at the end of the tunnel. Yes, yes, the light at the end of the tunnel.

Contents

Projection Machine

Barbello

In the beginning, there was a sudden gasp of breath. The taxis continued to pick up strangers. There was a division in place names. Lofty skyscraper arms made a mess of garden sand.

On the first day, he planted his newborn baby in the soil. The second day, the newborn sprouted through the mud, its fresh face tarnished with neighborhood gossip. Bones collect at the edge of the sea. We trod the shore, searching for our fingertips and our lunar belts.

In the beginning, we felt like zombies after much rest. The second day, everyone looked like a film star. The inner skies opened parted mouths to whisper. The moisture of planets birthing smaller planets under the trees of larger planets.

Before skyscrapers, there was heat.
And in the gardens, moist air.
Before any of this, there was
the limited idea
of sentence

We found hermit crabs fucking the clams until all the pearls loosened themselves
onto the ocean floor

We found entire beached whales pressing on the beaches until the indentation of their
bodies created a snow angelic form

The name of the transcendent
remains hidden. The obvious
place to look for it is among
the vowels:

the rivalry between holly
and ivy –

     murder, resurrection

               the graveyard shifts
               to reminisce

the cult of Mary Gipsy
came to England
by way of poor Spanish pilgrims –
palm branches in their hands
copies of apocryphal gospels
in their wallets
and Aphrodite's scallop shells
stitched in their caps

               numbers shift – even, odd

        the feast began on the first new moon of the year –
             memory tidal

Poetry, since it defies scientific analysis, must be rooted in some sort of magic, and magic is
reputable. European poetic lore is, indeed, ultimately based on magical principles. Now it is
only by rarity of spiritual progression that poets make their lives magically potent in the
ancient sense.

he stabilized the calendar –
the lover told the liar to begin

the zodiac is believed to have originated
in babylonia from the tale of gilgamesh
      killing of the bull
      love-passage with the virgin
      adventures with the two scorpion men
      the deluge story
            Somewhere in Anchorage Alaska
            Exxon Valdez, Exxon Valdez

one of the cruelest aspects of conversation:
      the back pedal

                    He loses touch with his more
                   practical wife, once his muse
                       in another room
                       he sits carving
                       the single poetic theme

In the beginning, we pricked our arms with mint leaves. Hospitals sank into lifeblood. She steadied the second hand. The womb around outside.

On the first day, bridesmaids felt each other up in dressing rooms. They necked in the bathrooms.

In the beginning, left turns to exits. Entrance ramps and stars. The lights turn red. The turnpike goes on endlessly. We return to our families.

the parted mouth
of the sky widens
releasing windy
vowel sounds

solve et coagula

Love begins with a *bench:*

    (here I'm coming in secret
    barefooted
    to smell the beeswax)

                         Nous and Logos
                         belong together:
                         their union
                         is life

I ask the singer what the priest is singing.
He tells me it is a funeral dirge written
in the ancient Yi language.

                 (We like to play
                  at dying: there's our
                  unknown crime.)

                              the voice in the distance
                              is incomprehensible
                              but clear and beautiful

Girls her age
took new-edged blades
to cut in mourning
for these curls
of their soft hair

              she   without the art   of putting
              her   skirt over   her ankles

the figure of wisdom (which we
encounter frequently
in Gnostic systems) indicates
a relationship

he number can it god he: morning mist and you survive several fights about organizing
rhythms into bed sheets can you pick leaves in the desert or the alps

she vibe the last only if infinite ratio she: frozen only if confident, she pulses the coming
trains of Brooklyn   subway ride, afternoon   the way statues lift arms under early light
can you morning eavesdrop   only if they round salve maria   sal-vay maria
they left church steps in order to ring faces like ministers

mother: bertolli light   she grabbed on the fist full   vapor relic
out of the marches, veronica   the planets, they seem fidgety   like on bus seats

father: only to sleep five more times   only if they bottle horizon
and we grow a bit after fighting   they hope for starfishing   night   night
night   night   night   surround the population embraces

mirror

I write this way because it happened to me. We act this way because it happened to us. Trees are not gentle. They push themselves through earth. Push themselves past sky.

I write this way because it happened long ago. I see tree outline framework. I feel indignation tree bark feasting empty sky. Trees used to be sky. Unfortunate tree breakages in the sky.

I write this way because it happened to me. The trees bring language up, vertical, above the complacency of soil. Language makes false stories about what happened, long ago, when I was barely beneath sky.

It happened to you, too. Remember. You'll get mad when you remember.

We were all children once. Before our first utterance, we learned pollen language. We learned to speak of trees, and how they rupture vast expanse. Later, we learned the silence of not speaking of trees, to keep hush the vultures of every morning when they plant sycamores upright. We feel the sting of pollen against our brushed playboy stomachs. The sting of tree bark on our thighs. The opening of soil to plant milk seed. The vibration/tug of earthworm in mud.

It happened long ago. I have no visible proof. Fathers leave traces of mud. I understand your mother hides in forests and she opens wide when the trees grow dark. I understand that you lost yourself there, too. I understand that you denied your walk through the forest and saw it later as a brisk walk at the start of day. But it was really night that time and there have been other times in similar state parks when you saw the outline of wildlife against the moon. And you denied that sight and later thought you had only seen the hollow shadows of trees. Think again. You'll get mad when you remember.

I write this way because it happened to me. It also happened to you. We struggle with the way we act when we see the clamor of thistle in the mildew of how we keep ourselves hidden, in language, in the defrost of wishing to devour each memory of our still birthed yet alive robbing.

the one time we stopped
looking beyond the traffic
we could finally see our
two faces situated
beneath the embers
of streetlamps
this light dwindles
into discord
we couldn't form ourselves
into knitted funeral costumes
the way we did in ocean towns
this building could be the same
as the granite street
where we found ourselves
more deciduous trees

        drape earthmasks
        like death sheets
        over the hardwood floor

there is a security checkpoint
at La Guardia airport
you are in a taxi
pulling away

        he never loved
        another person
        the way he loved
        the ceramic washing bowl
        she hid underneath
        her bed

Each time opposition is set up to make sense, the couple is destroyed. A universal battlefield. Death is always at work.

The morning after
I had to read several books
to forget the night before
     In my copy of Otto Rank's *Doppelganger*
     all of the important pages
     stuck together
          I thought I had spring-cleaned
          his sperm
          from my dress
               sitting cross-legged
                    the irony was that
                    cross-legged sitting
                    breaks the flow of blood
                    to the brain

                              I will never know
                              what it's like
                              to wake up beside myself
                              (o how I loved her
                               her fingers felt
                               just like mine)

a candle next to a hurricane
fire won't save
the avenue from flooding

Norea told Noah to pack his bag and build a ship. She took her two favorite giraffes, one male, one female. He took two llamas – one male, one female. They had two children – one male, one female. Noah was male and Norea female. The morning after, the rest of the world was gone and Norea told Noah
          that in the jungles, many animals
             used sexual intercourse
                as a means of saying hello
                    as well as farewell

one male

     and one female

The morning after

              I could only look in the mirror

                              lovingly

in my copy of Otto Rank's *Doppelganger*,
      there is a photo
      of a woman
      with long black hair

the morning after   we left   our spaces   in line   for personal development
my lips settled   like two lovers meeting   we passed the funeral department
we went down to floral   we went to the jewelry counter   settled upon a nice
death ring   to bring us closer   to warning   our memories need a lunar eclipse
to guide them into knowing

           the morning after
           I ran toward you with a death wish
           and I noticed you looked
           just
           like
           me

She Who Measures

No one refrains, in musical
      crescendo – like leap
         year, the moment advances:

           she is in the stitching room
           sewing new mermaid skin

the ocean is a mirror
and tidal waves
a cityscape

           in the trolley car
           he strained to see out
           the Bermuda flier-ed
           windows, many
           bayonet yards passing,
           many fig trees
           many nether clocks

a young commercial actress
goes to the back of the car
for a seat

        Fallen
           Fallen
       Flown

But in this way all of our atoms can celebrate their unified categorization. The Hoorah. In March, the sidewalks seem less alarming – snow begins to melt and not as many people fall over their own fever-feet. In Philadelphia, working class men drag up. They wear huge colorful masks and parade down Broad Street.

but parades
go on endlessly
without traffic
the endless ongoing sound
of rhythmic honking

two eight   six twenty three   ninety nine   eighty five   one billion and
two

sexophile   xenophobe   maria crusader, salve regina   sal-vay regina

we can't lift up the sheets   no more tonsils in the hound hooves   no listen
a bit more closely   they are protesting the end of salt

parades go endlessly and the streets serpentine for millions of years. I forgive him for
forgetting my stop.
The cab driver does not want to take me to East New York. He says it's too dangerous for a
girl. I tell him he's being both racist and sexist. He rolls his eyes and demands I get out of
the car.

> Dream thrum:
> Hum

He, the philosopher, said "you are yourself and nothing more and no matter where you go
you'll always remain."

Hermes Trismegestes brought the emerald tablets to the alchemists. He wanted to turn
slaves into gods. The alchemists, blinded by materialist principles, decided they would turn
lead to gold instead. At the center of the Earth, they surmised, is a storehouse (wasteland)
of precious metals. The trick is to get the center of the Earth without getting stuck there.
Venus is the Viking planet. Mercury is where Hermes lives. The sun creates lighthouse.

```
----------there are stars
      ---------that make lights
                    ------------on earth, we see them
                       ----------from the highway
             -----------------and call them
                    --------------------cities
```

now we hear
the locomotive
behind us, it's a winter sun
mixing with a truant
storm, it keeps
the path predecessor
to gang plank, rupture

with lack of glass we come up no more glue to paste sun to sky no more slang talk we can be
in the same rule book if we take one word out and give some space to grieve the sky to torch
five songs no songs the day we left our trace we moved our souls to a place we can speak to

memory like a lost amulet

      subject at the bottom of a hill

memory like I miscarried my child

      subject running through my head over and over again

memory in the promised land

      subject destroyed any chance for peace

memory like the crown will find an heir

      subject like the distance appropriate

memory played the whole night through

      subject had no benches

memory hadn't come up with anything yet

      subject would not allow us to get our clothes

memory like the bones can't cry

      subject like the pleas of black clad dancers

memory like a hall that leads through to the courtyard

      subject put his weapons on a pyre

memory stayed in five star hotels

      subject like the shady path leading up to the dome

memory conveniently having a reunion

      subject becomes accidentally in a stranger's body

on scales, we lavender light
forget dismal   many years
e s p I can predict
the last time right away
walked into the wrong movie
theater your eyes are filled
with torment

            in wishing ponds, I can't
            forget   brisk triumph
            zippered-shut, forget
            not to crush us under
            the water wheels
            that move round despite
            the click-clack
            vernacular drainage
            pipe

It takes a million years to count to one. It's a circus, they say, since we bought four dollar towels to dry the land of its crypto-chrism. We try to make it through, open-eyed, trying to form into knots the hand-delivered packaging tape we'll use to keep together the parking lots grown recently vacant.

I asked her
questions she could
not answer with simple
words. Questions about
why birds
mate only in winter
or why the seven
seas seem more like
one continuous ocean. She
slapped her hands against
the table and told me
I should be more
indifferent about things.

              where the air
              meets the land:
                  a hybrid form
                        of atomic
                            madness/sadness

god knows how many time zones

We wanted to take the train to Africa to learn more about the zodiac. In Fishtown, Philadelphia's Irish neighborhood, one woman told me the zodiac was based upon principles of ancient Celtic tree lore. The Ogham Language. Her lover was named Ricardo, a graffiti artist who loved to stick needles in his arms. I've only ingested heroin once. I got sick and could feel my soul peel.

We learned more about the zodiac in the Italian Market than we did on our safari through backwater Louisiana. After a more general look at the lunar eclipse, we packed our bags and left. We left as if with wings. We pushed our dustpan underneath the bed.

We wanted to take the train to Zimbabwe, specifically, to search for silver. Only once did we actually make it out of Boise. We fell several times out of the century train rides require for motion. We made hoops around the Midwest. We ended up several times in Kansas City, lamenting the pinkish hue the sun creates around the meager skyline.

For gold, we traveled west, beyond the swamps and swimming pools and found golden lanterns hanging above silver lampposts. The bronze age came years before we counted pennies at the Bank of America on 17th street. We sent away for postcards and felt rain in the postage stamps.

We took the bus to New York City to understand the waistlines of submarines and tanks. The machines lift weary mechanisms above the city. We continually hide behind the Chrysler Building until there is little left besides barbecues in the back lots. We have an audience now, everyone can see how much time it takes to declare a funeral.

Pulse. Low.

      Lower.

           there's no gold there
                 there's a forest
       there's no water there
                 sea salt loosens paper weights
       there's no harlequin dancer there
                 I wanted to seed one
       there's no vestal virgin there
                 I wanted to plant one
       there's no time there
                 just congratulation
       there's no sunlight there
                 the road is long

He told me we'd go to Albany.
    We left. Philadelphia grew smaller behind us.
                (Pennsylvania was founded by Quakers.
                Knowing this somehow made us feel
                safer. Like we'd
                grown up
                with simplicity.
                Like we'd grown up soundless
                      waiting for only the moved
                      to speak.)

the map on her bedroom wall
       slowly slides down:

                those countries

                                 hate her

as though Genghis Khan
redrew her forest
with leaves from Outer
Mongolia, placed
pigeons outside
her bedroom door,
a collection
of skyscrapers

But first, Mongolia – vanish. Multiply your beaches for our swimmings.
Very brightly, the sunbelt voracious, we slide hands along the atlas, find new places to live.

On the beach, we found plants that felt like summer. Only when we placed them on our
faces, they grew colder. And without them, we felt our journey lose itself in its last nerve.

gipsy sense sapient underbrush
cashmere doom fundamental
the islands full of hail storms
locoweed meiosis
Precambrian rehearsals
this way

In the museum halls of Westminster Abbey
       a curator talks to an American tourist
             about the death of John F. Kennedy
The curator went and bought a black dress upon learning of the death of the American Irish-
Catholic president. She was so used to wearing white. She said she couldn't sleep much that
night.

I place my last nerve in a bottle, send it floating down the river.

                In Rome, my family sits basking in too much sun, watching
                the Pope canonize a turn of the century
                village monk. The Pope spreads thick frankincense
                everywhere. My mother says the monk is our distant cousin.
                He lived on Mt. Verna and healed the village sick.

She gets stuck in Kansas for five hours. The road is hard. The woman in the town shop says she loves living in Kansas. Last year she got stuck in Pembina North Dakota en route to Saskatchewan.

Holy place:

the mirror

---becomes the land------------------------

There is one woman who is alone

                          There is another woman who is afraid

both glare at each other in the subway car

she flips through the latest issue
of *Harper's Bazaar,* glancing
at the latest in navy-style jackets

the one who is afraid
gazes out the subway
window

                the doors open
                a mechanical voice announces
                "Girard Avenue"

the one who is alone makes her way past the crowd
the one who is afraid stays inside the car
she picks up a copy of *The Philadelphia Inquirer*
and searches for the horoscope section

regicide in Valencia
wolfhound Zoroaster abandons amnesia
half sister
hypermedia
the lake district majestic
the prayer book a result of rhyme
Roanoke Virginia tantra
like the unparalleled unstuck

                thank you for clarifying
                the moment with
                splash tongue
                      fisting
                                sliding down
                between covers there was
                a certain drip
                        like longitude

nail ourselves onto the cobblestones of earlier cities
glue ourselves to each little pebble of the marketplace

        zarathustra street walks progesterone
        utopia individuates adonai
        manhattan archon crypto chrism
        voodoo flip flop sacrifice

we felt lonely the first time we saw him
peering through the jungle at the silver screen

we continue to move despite those forces that intend to keep us here forever

pretend the night is drapery enough for the unsung portions of the day to seem unimportant
despite how one can stand against the afternoon long enough to pretend the year is over --
each day damming up the one before

I don't want to see myself in the earlier city. For some believe the old must rip apart earth
mines. You become an honest watchtower. I am an angel with two voices. I sleep among
newspapers. At least he is a man. At least she is a woman. Created like larva, twisting in
subgum.

piled pearls – I could sell
an entire arms load for sheep
and manage to make enough profit
before morning

especially if we started
digging in the winter
we'd pull turnips
out of their graves
and almost be moved
to die in the earth
with them

my saint, you are brother in this land
and for that reason, I feed you straw
and allow you to sleep
in my slumber room

we shouldn't leave
so hesitate:

in earth years, the moon
bursts out of its shell
and replaces creation
with the slight ginger ringing
of bells

Only the bathroom is private.
I lock myself in for peace.

don't try
to forge
this new
don't try
to come from
don't
this space

We emerge dripping
from the river
holding two sounds
one like silver

SOPHIASLOGOS

Only the symbolic, a new signifier, can change the dominant law.

You can only go as far as walking will take you

we are moving, in Philadelphia   if you bare the agony, we draw the city's streets
she wore murals on her face   tool box he carried polyhedrons   a triangle
is the sum of its parts   half sister, we drew her into fragments   gipsy
sense   lunar eclipse   turn off the lamp   subway ride   here in the radius time
becomes circumference   after hoyt schermerhorn and bedford nostrand you feel a split
he cut her in two until the journey fragmented   no, we are not new york we are not san
francisco we are not 2nd avenue   you, beneath the waterfall you, closing the lights,
soft juniper   regicide   the throne is all malaria, Lassa Fever   Maiden Wire, calendars
hung on tiny nails   back bone   she had string in her hands making knots,
calvary winds pass and the urge to know summoned feelings kept in spine   time enough,
her lucid singing makes rowboats disappear   we are moving, under the awnings of
neon deli signs   we are moving, in a train through Zimbabwe   we are moving
through Bangladesh   jewelry counter, two silver necklaces and clasps
each and every starfish in the harbor fell into an opening chasm of sea dust   father
please give me motion enough   so I can face these earth toys   ministerial organ
death hum: thrum   real order   regicide   plague you

spider plants: we spread our arms to cover child's spills   she places her milk, like the
open sky, on harmony before sunday   she relaxes the silence between water and milk

He sets up navy yards. They fight over her sea. I can only see him stand up. Other times,
in the back corners. She would carry. Over the last moment. She would drag. I could only
see him looking down. Other times, in the alleys. He said the toolbox is a sum of its parts.
He pulled out his hammer, started constructing the earth. He put in pieces of mirror.

Open to tell the wilderness, unfurled, the poison is the spring is the jungle is the beach town
bush

out of her mouth flew the planes of Russia   Sundials over the desert and we cry Arizona
the margins between Prince Street and Canarsie. We opened the doors. She was mechanical
and whispered   most often, a slip   most often, we hang calendars with tiny
nails

Doppelganger: addition   we rule out the other   we can project millions of tables and
chairs   you repetition   we can million project chairs and we can million tables this chair

Aurora borealis blessed virgin cable vision television, sonora delight this spring your many
visigoths lie in the birth room flowering empty-handed genitalia. Such delight there is sweet
sonora what a star we are when we stand flat along living room walls. Bless you cable vision
television. Bless the desert with lies of water. Bless the harpoons of the hills. Several
soldiers hide in trees. Bless you Mayor Michael Nutter. Once nativity, wax dolls remove
parkas speak in anointed tongues.

like lions like megalomania   like arbitrary halloo   like natural language
they prison toe   we semen flow the calculated years   we hang our semen with
nails

His voice through loudspeakers. We hear him in our heads. Kyrie domine. He feels her in
the leaves. She spills out crustaceans. When his key ring disappeared they questioned the
military. The judge and coordinator of the army came and commanded, "you must untie
your ships and undock."

before we hang lamps over highways airplanes hang over the tired infinite standing sea
before gipsy sense they left the old ones and grabbed sky time with calendar hush, they
rolled abacus beads further along the yellow line

like Mendel's law we imperfect our diaphanous muck a muck   imperative downturn
we imperfect diaphanous   we move away from breeding

before the glitter bags fall into the palms of virgins. we destroy glory but only if they salve
maria, sal-vay maria. can you barrier the ocean   can you dam up

lord chancellor Nazarene unraveling   enraptured fireweed issachar   sheep skin
grace note   corpus juris   vernal seraphim   Padua warmonger
merchantmen   oracular equinox out and out

it gets so hard to speak in a roomful of darkness, yet the lights come on, and there's
a roomful of noise: vibrato wavers lake   feed famine plague trees

six million times to lay your boat on marshy land   cesspool   sod enough earth benching
break through mud, waver or plant six children in desert sand   wear crowns tilt felt hats
silver eldorado   fire can't be smog   candles can't be ancient moss

its time to rest. alabama, rest. saulsalito, rest. keep giving tides to charity. your dream, seven lobsters crawl toward the united states charity building. it's a vice to steal. O fallen grab basket cathedral. Let us carry your grocery carts past this time frame – seven past eight, quarter to four. A full clock twist. A seven, eight lunar dial.

undermine: under lanterns, streets shine and harbors shine and all clouds mysteriously amber untangle the stolen goods of miserly wombat politicos

relief relief relief san quentin   relief design prison doors

relief. we project millions of tables and chairs. you repetition. we project millions of:

basket weavers clamoring to basket the earth. tidal spring wood around the whole world. O clamor to keep our planet wooden. twigs on each ocean front. a wicker basket steeple. wooden men. silver people. golden henchmen who razzle dazzle television strings holding earth womb milk basket gravy chain.

remember dream lags wore down to coal mining   meet beside the golden trees
there are precious metals there: hesitate before mating season. stars don't mate
in their beds. they wilt or rejuvenate.

several prayers later and still no abraham still no naval yards   lined up, they quicken
their holy moses until fifty oceans meet cajoling

He placed precious metals under the earth. You repeat: he picked up his hammer, started constructing the earth.

you repetition –
        of bastard lands,
        such carnivals, rye fields,
        fool hardy in airport waiting areas, zen archery,
        the solemnity of mary this Saturday so I perfume my feet,
        gipsy sense, sky time,
        such calendar hush in many mansions, ha shem,
        proton mysterion, malillumination

you repetition –
  Burlingame. ocean lapping waves lapping eternal vowel sounds

repetition –

  in the beginning, in the end, he turns her clock-mast, time controlled, weather
  device and clears room for calvary winds to pull down streets so vibrantly

  on the last day, we collapsed inward, noticed perigee, and heard earth mites singing
  in death row chamber-ed cars

  on the last day, we vanished until cyclones lifted their blueprint memories, you
  repetition,   the final day,
                          we birthed wings, out wheel
                        out ///// oracular equinox
                            vernal seraphim

dry up your seaweed laden lottery numbers   you have approval to move despite those
forces that intend to lock you in your orchard yard   your hands quickly aging
many mansions   alive like never before

you repetition:

              under the ocean
              looms the last vagrant
              mirror grown dark

through visions, rotation

I repetition:

photo by Francesca Costanzo

Debrah Morkun believes in near death experiences and prays to the old gods. She toys around with magic and the coin toss, attempting to synthesize the two into holy orders. She resides in the city of brotherly love, and is a founding member of The New Philadelphia Poets.

Made in the USA
Charleston, SC
21 March 2010